CW00501736

SLOW HOMESCHOOLING

Short Essays About Mindful Homeschooling

By Milva McDonald

All rights reserved. No part of this publication may be reproduced, distributed, or transmitted in any form or by any means, including photocopying, recording, or other electronic or mechanical methods without the prior written permission of the author except for brief quotations embodied in critical reviews.

© 2017 Milva McDonald

ISBN: 9781521817353

Contents

INTRODUCTION

I've been homeschooling for a very long time. Since 1991, to be exact. The world has changed a lot since then, and homeschooling has changed drastically. Besides the obvious technological advances which have affected everyone and everything, numbers of homeschoolers have increased rapidly.

There are good things that go along with that. These days when people hear that you homeschool they're much more likely to know someone else who does it, or at least have read about it. While stereotypes still abound, homeschooling has become more commonplace.

Computers and the internet make communication easier in some ways, and less personal in others. E-lists and Facebook groups are a long way from the paper newsletters support group members lovingly created every month back in the day, but they do let us connect instantly. Online discussions are all over the place, eliminating the need for support group meetings. Still, talking to someone on the computer isn't the same as meeting in real life, and to forge connections, build partnerships, and grow friendships, people need to actually be with each other. It's ironic that during this time when more and more people are homeschooling, new families I talk with have a harder and harder time finding meaningful connections. The landscape is wider and more diffuse. E-lists and online group memberships swell with people who have little to do with each other. The lists become clearing houses for information on products and classes and field trips, and while that can certainly be useful, in my experience people are still longing to find friends and community for themselves and their children.

Now that we're a critical mass, we've become targets for businesses and product creators. The options for purchasing curriculum materials, signing up for classes at local museums and institutions of learning, hiring tutors catering specifically to homeschoolers, or enrolling your kids full or part-time in free standing drop-off learning centers that market to homeschoolers are staggering. Public schools have even gotten in on it, and in many states offer enrollment in public virtual schools, enticing homeschoolers by offering free computers and other perks. While students enrolled in these publicly funded options are not legally homeschoolers (they're on the rolls as public school students and must comply with all the requirements and testing that goes with that), they never step foot in the actual school building.

I am all for diversity in education and more choices for people. At the same time, when many families begin to homeschool they're often not just trying to figure out what works for their families. They're also inexperienced, nervous, and worried about doing a good job. They're malleable. Those who come to homeschooling because of a carefully researched philosophical position are less likely to buy reams of curriculum or enroll their kids in drop-off options, but more often than not, families come to homeschooling because their kids are having problems in school. Got materials that cover school-defined learning standards, or an alternative learning center that helps relieve parents' fears about teaching and socializing their kids, and you'll likely find some takers.

It wasn't that long ago that these options weren't available. We had to figure things out for ourselves, and that journey turned out to be one of the most rewarding of my life. People should make use of resources that work for them, but as with any act of consumption, carefully considering the necessity and ramifications makes for more mindful, meaningful living.

The writings in this book were written over a period of years, and first appeared on my blog, www.apotlucklife.com. They're not in chronological order, so references to my kids' ages will be non-linear and varied. They represent things I learned in my years of homeschooling, and celebrate the lifestyle which I call Slow Homeschooling. That lifestyle is about trusting your kids, enjoying time with them, building a community, and making the world and everyday living your classroom. The pieces are always short, and range from offering practical advice to waxing philosophical. I hope you enjoy them.

Slow Homeschooling

My homeschooling journey began 26 years ago, when my oldest daughter was attending public kindergarten. Like many parents, I was delighted that my little girl was growing up and entering school. I hoped she would make friends, learn a lot, and enjoy herself. It wasn't long before I realized I'd been carrying around an idealized vision of school. I began to explore options, and came upon a transcript of a speech by former New York City teacher of the year John Taylor Gatto[1]. Reading it changed my life. I committed myself to homeschooling.

There were about eight families at the first homeschooling picnic I attended. I felt inspired. These people were as excited about homeschooling as I was. Sure there weren't many of us, but we didn't really need more than we had–our families, each other, and the world to explore in any way we chose. Compared to today's homeschooling landscape, it wasn't much, but it was okay. In fact, it was more than okay. We weren't homeschooling because homeschoolers perform better than average on standardized tests, or because there was a great

[1] John Taylor Gatto, Dumbing Us Down: The Hidden Curriculum of Compulsory Schooling

network in our area, or because we were grooming our kids for the Ivy League. We were doing it for perhaps the best reason of all–because we had to. The promise of freedom for our children and our families was too good to resist.

Fast forward to 2017. The changes in the homeschooling movement since I began make my head spin. Homeschoolers in the United States now number in the millions. In my local support group alone, there are more than 200 member families. Museums, nature sanctuaries, art studios, and all manner of places now offer daytime classes for homeschoolers.

The families who contact me regularly to ask about homeschooling can choose the groups they like best, and the classes and programs they want to use to tailor their children's educations. Want a scheduled activity every day of the week? No problem. How wonderful, in many ways, that homeschooling is becoming more accepted, and that homeschoolers can now choose from such a wide range of options, including learning centers for homeschoolers. Usually these centers are professionally run, offering part-time or even full-time drop-off options. What a difference from my early days, when our small group of families made our own fun. Libraries, playgrounds, museums, historic sites, the great outdoors, and each other's houses–we explored them all, when we decided, when we chose. We created our own field trips, started our own clubs, planned our own potlucks, put on our own plays, and if we felt like it, offered or organized our own classes. Although I can certainly see the positive aspects in all the resources now available to homeschoolers, I wouldn't have had it any other way.

I know there are still families who practice the kind of homeschooling I'm discussing here, but when I talk to new homeschoolers, their attention is inevitably drawn to all the available resources. Creating complex schedules that fill children's time with classes, lessons, and days spent at drop-off learning centers takes the place of free play, unplanned trips to the library and park, baking cookies together, or snuggling up on the couch to read picture book after picture book. With my older kids grown and out of the house, and my youngest the only one left at home, our lives are less like that. All my children are very scheduled, out in the world pursuing rich, full lives which are, in many ways, beyond anything I could have imagined for them. When they were still small, people astonished by their "skills" would ask me point blank, "What did you do?"

My answer was always the same: Nothing.

Why did I say that? Partly, because I was taken aback by the question. Really, I did nothing other than provide love, care, shelter, support, and fun. I observed my kids with interest and joy, and provided resources to help feed budding passions. I did my best to act as a guide while trying to stay the heck out of their way. What I did not do when they were very young was sign them up for every math workshop, science club, or whatever activity came on the homeschooling list serve, and I certainly never enrolled them in a learning center. It just wasn't necessary. Beyond a pottery session and a few music lessons here and there, for the most part structured classes and lessons weren't even a part of my kids' lives until they hit double digits.

So what did we do? We spent our time at the park, the library, and in play. I was active in homeschooling and community organizations, and the kids always tagged along to meetings, bringing stuff to do, working on their own projects alongside the adults at work. The whole family sang in a chorus together. We read lots of books. We went to, and sometimes performed in, concerts, plays, and museums. They especially loved the Museum of Fine Arts, where they'd wander through the galleries at their own pace, stopping when and where they chose to pull out their trusty sketch pads and render their own version of an awesome masterpiece.

To me, those were the golden days of homeschooling. I'm so grateful for the time we spent together, getting to know and love each other, enjoying the city, the beach, farms, museums, the woods, the playgrounds, and so many other things in the world around us. I never gave a thought to the teaching of reading, math, or any other academic pursuit, not because I didn't care, but because I didn't have to. The kids wanted to learn, and did so. It was the lifestyle, and all of the blessings and benefits that came with it, that I cared about.

Perhaps I make the lifestyle sound unbelievably idyllic. If so, it's because of how I remember it, not because there were no struggles or difficulties. Those come with any life choices. In my experience, what people worry about most when they start homeschooling are academics and socialization. I wasn't immune to those worries (parents whose kids are enrolled in school don't escape them, either). Back in the good old days of homeschooling, we had the time, the space, and the opportunity to work out those concerns ourselves, and we learned that, societal messages aside, our kids could, for the most part, thrive without structured activities or centers designed solely for the purpose of "educating" them or providing "self-directed" learning environments for them. We learned that the ultimate learning environment is life itself, no didactic trappings required. For me, one of the most important lessons was to savor life with my family.

Recently, I had coffee with a couple of other veteran homeschooling parents, and we discussed the influx of learning centers. Things are so different now, we noted. Better in some ways, true, since resources can allow families to homeschool who couldn't do so otherwise. But what of our experience, the way we homeschooled? Will it become a relic, now that homeschoolers are a significant market, and programs and centers designed for them are popping up fast and furious, touting their offerings, contributing to the notion that professionals of one sort or another are necessary?

Slow homeschooling is what we did, we decided. In our frenetic 21st century world, maybe it will become a fad that sticks, like the slow food movement. At the very least, we hope our experiences can serve as a reminder that choosing a less harried and more self-directed way of life is possible.

13 Things I Want You to Know About Homeschooling

1. Anyone can do it. "I could never do that" is a statement homeschooling parents hear all the time, but homeschooling isn't nearly so hard as many people think.

2. There's not one right way. Homeschooling is the ultimate individualized education. No how-to manual could begin to cover the myriad styles, approaches, and routines homeschooling families embrace.

3. Homeschooling doesn't mean sitting at home all day. Don't take the word "homeschooling" literally. Learning happens at the library, the park, the museum, the nature sanctuary, all over the place.

4. Homeschooling is a lifestyle. It's not just about how kids learn the three R's. It's about building relationships, cuddling up on the couch with a good book, spending lazy days at the beach, hanging at the museum for hours, exploring the community, and living in the moment.

5. Socialization is actually a plus. Because they're not age-segregated on a daily basis, homeschoolers are more likely to associate with people of varied ages. For a lot of parents, that makes socialization one of the benefits of homeschooling.

6. Homeschooling parents don't have to teach everything. Yes, we teach our kids a lot, but much of the time, we're acting as facilitators. We tap into resources on the internet, in the community, and beyond. And let's not forget the oft-overlooked fact that kids teach themselves quite a lot, too.

7. Homeschoolers are a market. From curriculum companies, to learning centers, to self-employed tutors, somebody's always trying to sell us something. More often than not, it's something we don't need.

8. Homeschoolers are a diverse group. The reasons people come to homeschooling are broad and varied, so don't make assumptions before getting to know us.

9. Homeschoolers enjoy time, space, and sleep. Our kids have lots of time to laugh, play, ponder, and create. Not getting enough z's isn't good for anybody, so the chance to get adequate rest is a boon.

10. Homeschoolers get into college. The Ivy League, private colleges, state schools, trade schools, you name it. They've all accepted homeschoolers.

11. Homeschooling is just another way to educate kids. Some kids go to public school, some go to private school, and some are homeschooled. Simple as that.

12. Homeschooling is good for society. Variety is the spice of life, and diversity in education makes our country a more vibrant, option-filled place to be.

13. Homeschoolers are all around you. We're at the playground, in the supermarket, at the library. We're in math clubs, on sports teams, in theater productions. Our grown-up kids are teachers, doctors, nurses, lawyers, carpenters, therapists, engineers, artists, and computer programmers. We're living our lives in the community, like everyone else.

Is Homeschooling Hard?

Oh, I could never do that. Most homeschooling parents have heard this after mentioning the way they educate their children. It has always seemed to me a strange response. For one thing, I'm never suggesting the other person do it. For another, homeschooling isn't all that hard.

There are plenty of societal messages that lead people to believe it is difficult, and these days, plenty of people and establishments cropping up to offer parents places to leave their kids that look a lot like school. For learning centers, alternative schools, educational day care centers, and places like them, encouraging the idea that homeschooling is hard is good for business. But is it true?

Nothing is without its difficulties, but homeschooling can make life easier in many ways. No more fights over getting out of bed in the morning. No more rushing to get to school on time. No more tearing your hair out trying to make sure your kids do their homework. Problems like bullying, anxiety, depression, and lack of interest in learning can also disappear.

So what are some of the myths that make people think homeschooling is hard?

Educating kids requires trained experts Let's face it, education is big business. Schools employ scores of people, and while teachers may not be getting rich, thanks to standards based education, corporations are. For the entrenched school system to continue to survive, and for newer initiatives like Common Core and mandatory testing to take hold, the overarching belief must be that children need trained experts to teach them. When schools fail, the general response is to insist that kids need even more time with trained experts. Longer school days and mandatory preschool have become a rallying cry for many who insist that children need school, and lots of it, to get a decent education. Homeschoolers reject these notions, operating under a different paradigm, one that values children's natural curiosity and drive to learn.

Spending time with kids is no fun Our culture is steeped in the idea that parents can't wait to get rid of kids. The media is filled with images of moms and dads filled with relief at back to school time. We're just not supposed to want to spend too much time with our kids. If we do, we're accused of helicopter parenting, overprotectiveness, or trying to live through our children. It is true that to homeschool, you have to want to spend time with your kids, but doing so isn't a burden. It offers us the opportunity to know our children well, develop strong relationships with them, and enjoy a more relaxed lifestyle centered around living and learning together.

Kids won't learn unless you make them This myth goes alongside the idea that kids are lazy. It's simply not true. Human beings are innately curious, which means they have an innate capacity for learning. Trying to make kids learn things they don't want to learn, aren't ready to learn, or don't see any reason to learn–yes, those things are hard. Exposing them to a wide range of subjects, honoring their natural curiosity, providing resources, supporting their passions, and tapping into community opportunities make life, learning, and even hard work seem more like a piece of cake.

Kids have to be with other kids The idea that homeschoolers don't have opportunities for socialization is a common myth. Support groups, community organizations, lessons, sports teams, volunteering, internships, jobs, you name it–the opportunities for homeschoolers to be out in the world with other people are boundless. And yet, the age segregation of schools has led many to believe that kids must be with children of the same or similar ages on a regular basis. As a result, new homeschooling families sometimes bend over backwards to try and connect their kids with agemates. Eventually, most get over that and discover that it's easier to enjoy the benefits of age-mixing.

College is a requirement Most parents stress about whether and where their kids are going to get into college. We want them to be able to go to any school they choose, but we also assume that college is a must. Homeschoolers get into college all the time, but the belief that they'll be disadvantaged is still common and contributes to the idea that homeschooling is hard. Homeschoolers who want to go to college do, but for many, the experience of having been alternatively educated opens their minds to other choices.

While homeschooling requires commitment, it doesn't have to feel hard. For many, it feels like a rewarding, worthwhile effort that can be done without the aid of learning centers and other entrepreneurial start-ups that target homeschoolers. Still, all the suggestions and reassurance in the world won't help you if you can't find a way to trust that you are doing what's right for your family, and that your child is competent and capable of learning. If homeschooling is important enough to you, you'll stick with it. If not, hopefully you'll find what's right for you, no guilt or shame necessary.

Just Like a homeschooler

I sing in a chorus, and after one of our recent concerts, my daughter chatted up the percussionist.

"She's a networker," pointed out one of my fellow choristers. The woman was impressed, but to me it was nothing new. "That's just like a homeschooler," I thought to myself. Like many young people who are home educated, my daughter isn't uncomfortable in social situations, and she likes meeting and talking with people.

It got me thinking about the characteristics of many thriving homeschoolers I know. At the risk of indulging in generalizations, here's my list. I don't think of these as absolutes. Rather, they're my commentary on the potential of homeschooling, the reasons I homeschool, and my personal wish list for my kids.

Confidence Yeah, I know talking about self-confidence and self-esteem can reek of cliché. They're still right up there with the qualities I want to cultivate in my kids. How does homeschooling help? Read on and you'll get the idea.

Intrinsic motivation Homeschoolers are more likely to do things for reasons that come from within. While homeschoolers certainly strive to excel, their pursuits are grounded in a desire to learn, and a love of the subject or activity at hand. I've seen how this has helped my own kids withstand criticism and weather the times when their hopes aren't fulfilled. When the flame burns from within, criticism doesn't cause discouragement or setbacks. On the contrary, it becomes another useful tool in working toward improvement.

Curiosity Remember the inquisitive toddler who drove you crazy wanting to know everything about everything? When kids are not shuttled from one subject to the next on an hourly basis, made to sit through day after day of classroom lectures and activities, and forced to complete reams of schoolwork that's often unconnected to their lives, that kind of zest for knowledge and intellectual curiosity remains blessedly intact.

Social savvy Yeah, I know that "What about socialization?" is one of the biggies when it comes to the general public's doubts about homeschooling. Oh, the irony. The fact is, homeschoolers can have a big advantage in the socialization department. Homeschoolers can spend lots of time in the community mixing with people of all ages, and are spared from dealing with excessive amounts of peer pressure.

Self-knowledge To thine own self be true can be easier said than done. Homeschoolers have a leg up. Why? They haven't spent their childhoods being graded, evaluated, and told what they're good at by educational professionals. Instead, they're free to learn at their own pace, experiment with different ways of learning, and figure out how to expand on their strengths and address their weaknesses. They also have more time to spend in solitude, a crucial component of developing self-awareness.

Joie de vivre All that play, social interaction, and pursuit of passions makes for a happy person. I don't know about you, but for this mom, that makes it all worth it.

Getting the Most Out of Your Support Group

What about socialization? It's a question often heard by homeschooling parents, but experienced homeschoolers know it's a non-issue. Social opportunities for homeschoolers abound. One of the best ways to take advantage of the wealth of available resources is to join a support group.

Some groups are loosely organized networks, while others are structured in a more hierarchical fashion. Some are open and inclusive, while others cater to particular educational philosophies or beliefs. Families often join more than one. For those wondering how to make the most of a homeschool support group, a few suggestions follow.

Don't forget the face to face Virtual support groups and e-lists abound, but there's no replacement for getting together with others on a face-to-face basis. Look for groups with less e-list chatter and more opportunities for real time activities.

Participate! Those group activities and classes you're enjoying were likely organized by a volunteer. Most groups depend on members to keep things vital and rolling. Think about what you can offer and put it out there. Whether it's hosting a group meeting or potluck, teaching a class, organizing a science fair, or planning a field trip, becoming an active member of the group is a great way to make the programs you want happen, meet new friends, and help others.

Don't be shy Breaking into a new group can be tough for anyone. Do your best to introduce yourself and feel free to ask questions about homeschooling, and about how things work in the group you've joined. Even a virtual introduction on a list serve can help you connect with others who may share your interests and goals.

It takes time You finally make it to the playground with your kid, and it seems that no one is paying any attention to him. Worse yet, it feels like the parents are chatting happily with each other and completely ignoring you. First, take a deep breath. These parents and kids are at a group event enjoying each other, as you would be—and probably will be—once you get to know everyone. Introducing yourself, sharing your interests, and contributing to the group will all help speed up the process.

Practice Tolerance Homeschooling parents tend to be an opinionated lot. Views on parenting and education are bound to differ among families in any support group. If conflicts arise, do your best to stay true to your own principles while acknowledging that others may have different views.

Whenever possible, let kids handle their own social struggles As homeschooling parents, we're often well acquainted with the families of our kids' friends. This doesn't mean we should butt in when our kids are experiencing issues with them. Growing up is a thorny business. Our children are learning how to communicate effectively in relationships. While it's easy to jump right in and get involved, sometimes the best way to help is to just listen. This is especially true when we're parenting teenagers.

Where are those groups? For more info on local groups in your area, ask your state homeschooling organization.

Can You Work and Homeschool?

In many homeschooling families, parents create a division of labor in which one works full time and the other stays home with the kids. While this may be the most obvious set-up for homeschooling, it's not the only option. Single parents and families with two working parents also homeschool quite happily. Below are ideas for making homeschooling work when you have to work.

Be flexible When both parents want or need to work, seek non-traditional employment situations. I have a part-time job that offers a semi-flexible schedule I fulfill partially at the office and partially at home. My husband is a musician with a flexible schedule and his hours fall mostly on afternoons, evenings, and weekends. Did you find the key word in that? It's *flexible*. If there's any way you can find a job with flexible hours you'll have an easier time creating a workable homeschooling schedule. The other situation that's advantageous for homeschooling is the ability to work at home.

Who's the boss? Another option is to be your own boss. Homeschooling parents have been known to start their own businesses and hence make their own hours. Fields I've seen work for people include child care, catering, teaching, editing, dog walking, and web design. That's not an exhaustive list, of course. Follow your passion, something you may feel more inspired to do once you see how homeschooling allows you to let your kids follow theirs.

Assess your options Creativity and cooperation are your friends in this endeavor. Sit down with your partner and brainstorm. Can either of you work different hours? Fewer hours? Work at home? Take your children to work with you? Can you take turns working? In one family I know, the dad works for a few years, then the mom takes a turn. When my teenager was an infant, I worked at night and brought her to the office with me. The key here is keeping an open mind and understanding that once you start thinking outside the box, you do have options.

Use the village What if you're a single parent and don't have a partner with whom to negotiate this territory? Or, what if you're in a situation where there are hours during the week when both parents simply have to be at work? In cases like this, look to your homeschooling support group. Often, you can find another homeschooling family willing to work with your kids on a regular basis for a fee or even barter. If your needs are sporadic, swapping child care is an option. Sometimes, the solution involves several families helping each other with rides, kid watching, and more. Figuring out a schedule that offers your child a satisfying homeschooling experience might not be simple, but it can be successfully done. Don't be afraid to ask for (and offer) help. Another obvious solution is hiring a teacher or tutor to be with your kids in your home while you're at work. While that may seem easier, it's far more costly and in the end, may not be as rich and rewarding.

Ask the kids Don't forget to involve your children in the discussion. They're stakeholders in the outcome, and they may have some great ideas for solutions, too. Remember that the window for needing someone to be with your kids while you work is relatively small. Each family has to make personal decisions about when kids can start staying home alone, but regardless of yours, in the scheme of a lifetime the period during which you'll have to juggle working and homeschooling is not long. Another payoff for doing it is that homeschoolers tend to be self-sufficient and independent, which makes homeschooling and working during the teenage years, when kids can get around on their own, even easier.

Making Our Own Kind of Music

Every so often I hear people ask the question, how do you unschool music? How do you learn music without lessons or instruction?

First off, unschooling doesn't mean you can't have a teacher, use instructional materials, or undertake any other kind of traditional study. By the same token, those methods aren't necessarily required to learn music. The trick is to foster appreciation for music, support whatever involvement in music your kids choose, and keep the joy and creativity in music making alive.

All four of my kids are musical in different ways. Kid one leaned toward the singer-songwriter world, number two embraces traditional folk, number three is a devoted jazz fan and vocalist, and number four likes classical best, although she also enjoys playing klezmer with her dad.

Below are some ideas for how to nurture musical intelligence in your kids.

Exposure First and foremost, expose your kids to many different kinds of music. There are plenty of excellent recordings made expressly for kids. By all means enjoy them, but play other music, too. As young children my kids loved Bob Dylan, Beethoven, The Beatles, Queen, other more obscure bands, and many kinds of ethnic music. Don't just listen to music around the house, go hear live music, too. I really can't overestimate the importance of exposure to music. My daughter is a perfect example. Our kids regularly attended classical, folk, and world music concerts, but we didn't go hear jazz very often, or listen to it much at home. That all changed when Ella Fitzgerald found her way onto the family mp3 player when my daughter was 11. She fell in immediate, absolute, obsessive love. Within months she had listened to and learned Ella's entire canon, mostly by taking her CDs out of the library, and today she's an accomplished, primarily self-taught jazz vocalist.

Modeling If you want your kids to learn about and love music, do it yourself. My husband is a musician, so our kids witnessed the joys of making music on a regular basis, as well as the necessity of practice. I'm an amateur singer and the kids listened to me practice choral music they later heard in performance. Even if you don't want to pick up an instrument or sing, you can still model music appreciation through listening and enjoying music yourself.

Make music together Since learning to listen is one of the most important aspects of making music, this is pretty important. One of the things our family did was sing in an intergenerational chorus and perform in intergenerational theatrical productions. If those kinds of commitments are more than you can handle, try seeking out (or organizing) low-key events like sing-a-longs, or folk, blues, or jazz jams. If classical music appeals, there's plenty of simple chamber music your kids can try with you or some friends. Ditto for rock and roll.

Find mentors No matter the undertaking, whenever my kids felt passionate about something, they found a mentor. With music, there's no reason that person can't be a teacher, especially if your child asks for lessons. All our kids took lessons on various instruments at one point or another, and were free to quit if their interest waned. Sometimes mentors are more like idols–masters your kids might never meet but nevertheless become huge influences, much like Ella Fitzgerald was for my daughter. My son found some of his musical heroes on YouTube, mandolin players like Chris Thile and singers like Tony Cuffe.

A word about practice This is a controversial subject, especially for unschoolers who might feel that "making" their kids practice is anathema. Because our family takes financial commitments seriously, and because my husband, as a music teacher himself, understands the vital role of practice in playing music, we did require our kids to practice as long as we were paying for music lessons they wanted. This doesn't have to be a rigid endeavor. Since the lessons were chosen by the kids, practicing mostly happened naturally, but if it didn't, we discussed the issue and negotiated agreements that worked for all. How practice works is going to look different in every family, but the key thing is to not squash a love of music by forcing the issue.

Resources Make instruments readily accessible to the extent it's possible. If you can get your hands on a piano, guitar, or other instrument, have them in your home. Recorders or penny whistles are inexpensive and easy to play. Don't discount percussion–rhythm is a huge part of music, and real or makeshift drums can be loads of fun. Whatever instruments you collect, let your kids experiment with them freely. Make CDs, records, downloaded music, or whatever technology you use to listen to music accessible, and offer a wide variety of music. When you go to the library, check out music in addition to books. Be musically curious, open-minded, and experimental, and most likely, your kids will be, too.

The Joys of Reading Aloud

We don't read out loud anymore. That statement was proudly delivered by another mom, whose kids had reached the milestone of being able to read books by themselves.

I don't minimize the importance of that milestone, and the joy that comes from curling up on your own with a good book. But I do lament the idea that the ability to read independently means reading aloud comes to an end.

My kids still at home are 18 and 16, and we still read together. It used to be books like *Little House on the Prarie*, the Harry Potter series, and *Finn Family Moomintroll.* These days, it's *The Count of Monte Cristo, Anna Karenina*, and *Mansfield Park.* They find it as enjoyable as ever.

Reading aloud is not something I do only with my kids. My husband and I like it, too. At the risk of sounding like an old fuddy duddy, I admit the following: I knit, he reads out loud. Recently, we've finished *Jude the Obscure, The Great Gatsby, Steppenwolf, Wise Blood*, and *Kindred*, and are part way through *The Goldfinch.*

Reading aloud is a great social activity, too. Every other week, we get together with other families for what we call *Read & Feed.* People take turns reading chapters, then we potluck, then we read again. We've been doing this for years. When the kids were little, we loved books like *The Prince of the Pond* and *Alice's Adventures in Wonderland.* As they got older, we tackled *Jane Eyre*, *The Portrait of a Lady*, and *Dracula.* The books are fabulous, and so is the feasting and the company.

As a homeschooling parent, you can choose to continue reading to your kids (don't forget to invite them to read out loud, too). You can also host social evenings that involve reading aloud. If you're not up for a novel, poetry is great, and reading a play aloud is loads of fun.

You can also start a book group with other homeschooling kids. If you do, remember to stay open-minded about what it means to pay attention. When my adult son was eleven, I hosted a group in my house. I read *The Neverending Story* aloud to about half a dozen boys. I vividly recall one of them acting out each scene as it was read. At first, my own preconceptions about how one is supposed to behave while listening caused me a bit of worry. But I decided to go with the flow, and realized that this kid's natural response was to be physical about what he was hearing. By doing so, he was processing the text more deeply. It wasn't a bit disruptive, perhaps because his behavior was coming from a place of connection with the book, and I think all the kids knew that. They were just as wrapped up in the story, and appreciated their friend's interpretation of it.

As far as the benefits of reading aloud, I can only theorize that a focus on listening to literature had something to do with my son's ability to nail, in less than 24 hours, reams of lines for a play in which he had the lead role. I can only guess that a lifetime of attentive listening makes reciting their favorite poems from memory, and learning speeches from Shakespeare plays, a snap for my daughters. I also wholeheartedly agree with those who think literature and stories are some of the best tools for learning about anything. But I can only say one thing with absolute certainty: reading great books aloud is totally fun. What more of a reason do you need?

The Benefits of Age-Mixing

Socialization is a concern homeschooling parents hear about all the time. Those of us who are seasoned homeschoolers know it's a non-issue.

In fact, the opportunities for mixed-age socialization is one of homeschooling's great benefits. At homeschooling park days, kids of all ages interact and play with each other. My teens attend one where some kids engage in a game of ultimate frisbee, while others play capture the flag, and still others enjoy the playground or brook.

Generally, it's teenagers who play ultimate frisbee, but an interested and motivated younger child would not be turned away. Sometimes, you can see younger children watching the game with rapt attention, clearly admiring the "big kids" and looking forward to joining their ranks. When a younger kid wants to be in the game, the older kids get to mentor them.

In recent years, I've noticed a tendency in homeschooling support groups to create events that are age-segregated. If these gatherings are a small part of a person's life, and the person is engaging in the larger world full of many different kinds of people, they can be just one component of a full life. But sometimes I feel like the push toward creating age-segregated events in homeschooling groups is driven by our cultural obsession with age segregation.

There's research on the benefits of mixed-age groups, but even without empirical evidence, my common sense and my own experience tell me that age-mixing is a better choice. We all gain knowledge, perspective, compassion, and confidence from interacting with people from all stages of life.

When older children serve as mentors and role models for younger children, either intentionally (by acting as a teacher, director, or tutor, for example), or inadvertently (by playing in their presence a robust game of ultimate frisbee that involves cooperation and skill), the benefits are tremendous. Adults also reap rewards from developing relationships with kids.

It's true that sometimes parameters need to be set for a group. Parents who want to start a math club might need to define the level of ability required to join. A writing group might necessitate a particular skill level to participate. In all these cases, homeschooling parents can consider ability rather than age as the most important criteria.

When my son was turning 16, the list of invitees for his birthday party included homeschooled and schooled kids ranging in age from toddlers to teens, homeschooling parents and other adults he counted as friends, and adult members of his birding group. The gathering reflected what I have seen to be true time and again — homeschoolers raised with plenty of mixed-age experiences become socially well-adjusted teens and adults who enjoy relationships with all kinds of people.

Interactions with people of all ages is something which homeschooling naturally offers, so get over the idea that classes, activities, and other programs need to be defined by age, and enjoy and reap the benefits of age mixing.

What Do Homeschoolers Do?

Homeschoolers number in the millions now, so why is it still so hard for people to understand what we actually *do*?

I know, of course, that there are so many ways of "doing" homeschooling. The ultimate individualized education, I like to call it, which means it's different for every family. Still, you'd think that stereotypical misconceptions, at least, would go away. I and my one child left at home regularly encounter them. We attend a lecture, and on the way out my daughter is asked if she'll be writing a paper on it the following day. We go to a social event, and someone inquires whether my daughter's schoolwork for the day is finished. She's reading a book, and the nice lady on the bus wants to know whether she'll be taking a test on it. Almost every week, I meet people who assume that I'm teaching my daughter everything, from biology to algebra to English.

Everyone is well meaning, and of course, why would someone understand something they haven't experienced? One problem is the word "homeschooling." For better or worse, it's the commonly used term for parents educating their children outside of schools, but it doesn't accurately describe what we do. Most of us are not recreating school in the home. Quite the contrary, much of the time we're out in the world doing things that don't remotely look like school. Parent-directed education is a better term.

When people make assumptions about how homeschooling happens they're often relying on stereotypes about education in general, i.e. traditional schooling, with the learner being spoon fed information by a teacher then tested and evaluated. That's only one model. Many people who choose not to send their children to school are choosing an alternate model, one that looks completely different from a traditional classroom. My kids, for instance, did not do structured schoolwork. They drew pictures, read books, made music, rode unicycles, created comics, played chess, wrote stories. They went to the park, the library, historical houses, museums, book groups, the beach, the woods, the theater. When my husband or I attended meetings, volunteered at soup kitchens, went to the supermarket, or voted, they tagged along. As they matured and entered their teenage years, they started enrolling in classes at community colleges, volunteering, and pursuing the interests they'd spent their childhoods developing.

By that time, it was easier to answer questions about homeschooling. I could just talk about the college classes, the volunteer jobs at the science museum and hospital, the performances in plays and concerts, or whatever. When they were younger and spending most of their time playing, dealing with well-intentioned folks assuming they spent hours a day being instructed by me was more challenging.

That antiquated outlook on education doesn't make sense. While the world has changed a lot over the last century, the school model hasn't. Materials and techniques perhaps have shifted, but the hierarchical structure and the philosophy that children must be compelled to learn remains the same. Technology, it seems, is shaking up that system at its core, offering options that have never been available and encouraging novel approaches to learning. At the same time, the drive for standards-based education entrenches the status quo more deeply, making it more rigid and inflexible, tying the hands of teachers and shunning innovation. How this will play out remains to be seen, but I for one would love to see what we now consider alternatives become nothing more than choices on a spectrum of normal. When we get to that point, the education revolution will have really happened.

Getting on Our Groove

It's Monday morning and we're all busy. My husband is doing paperwork before heading out to teach for the afternoon, I'm writing this article, my 18-year-old is making smoothies for breakfast, and my 16-year-old is awaiting the arrival of a bunch of teenagers for a rehearsal of a Shakespeare play. This afternoon, she'll get on the bus and head to a theater in the next town for another rehearsal. This evening, I'll go sing with my chorus while another crop of teens arrives at my house for a meeting of my 18-year-old's Model United Nations Club.

Sometimes I joke that our house is like Grand Central Station. There's always a steady stream of people coming and going for work, for play, for fun, for the business of life. This alive, dynamic lifestyle is, for our family, one of the best parts of homeschooling. Having two employed parents with flexible schedules may contribute to the winding nature of our days, but even in families with a more traditional set-up, homeschooling offers the opportunity to develop an organic rhythm, a groove that allows everyone to learn and thrive.

For me, simply making the decision to homeschool opened up doors of opportunity. Once I realized I didn't have to send my kids to school, other outside-the-box options I never would have considered before seemed possible. As time went by, my homeschooling lifestyle taught me that what I once would have considered absurd wasn't only real, it was desirable. I watched my kids learn to read with no formal instruction. I observed them taking an interest in numbers and figuring out how to add and subtract without prodding. Most of all, I learned that the more I stayed out of my kids' way, the more they blossomed.

Finding the rhythm that worked for our family involved a few key components. The first was play. From the time our kids were born they spent most of their time playing. Sometimes it would be at the park during a support group gathering, other times at friends' houses, and often outdoors. The curiosity and freedom of expression they enjoyed in play spilled over into everyday life. Baking cookies, for example, became a game, one that continued once the task was done at splendid tea parties where they could practice being grown-up, not just in behavior but in conversational topics, which included politics, child care, and whatever else they heard adults around them discussing.

Which brings me to another important component of our homeschooling. Our kids hung around with adults a lot, working and playing alongside them. They sang in an intergenerational chorus and performed in intergenerational plays, attended grown-up concerts and talks, and regularly tagged along to meetings for my volunteer work, or rehearsals of their father's band. They always carried books or art supplies or games to play while the grown-ups did their thing, but don't think for a minute that they weren't paying attention.

How did this integrated, play-oriented lifestyle benefit our family? It allowed our kids to develop self-sufficiency, for one thing. They learned at a young age how to occupy themselves, which renders obsolete one question commonly directed at homeschooling parents: *How do you find time for yourself?* Last summer, researchers at the University of Colorado Boulder reported that children spending more time in unstructured activities were better able to set goals and meet them without prodding from adults.[2] In the small sample size

---

[2] Less-structured time in children's daily lives predicts self-directed executive functioning; Barker, Semenov, Michaelson, Provan, Snyder, Munakata. Frontiers in Psychology, June 17, 2014.

of our family, that's certainly been the case. Through being in charge of their play and their learning, our kids learned to trust themselves, they became confident, and they discovered passions they pursue with gusto.

Guiding our kids to find those passions was one of the most important goals of our homeschooling, and engaging in a rich, bustling life which exposed them to lots of people and experiences was a big help. With the benefit of hindsight, I can see clues to the passions they'd later embrace peppered throughout my kids' lives, but watching the process unfold was full of surprises. My 18-year-old loved singing from the time she was a baby, for instance, and was always very social, but we had no idea she'd embrace jazz and psychology so fiercely. My 16-year-old watched her older siblings in plays and attended theater productions with us enthusiastically, but who'd have thought that when she was 13 she'd start her own theater company?

These discoveries are some of the gifts we receive as we watch our kids learn, grow, and become. When people say homeschooling is a lifestyle, that's what they mean. It's about flow, trying new things, connecting with each other and what we love, and learning all the time.

The Gift of Time

Last night I ran into a dad whose eldest had started homeschooling as a pre-teen and is now in her first year of college. I asked how she was doing. "Great," he replied. "Homeschooling really saved her. It gave her the time to pursue what she really wanted to do."

I nodded. The advantages of homeschooling are many, but if I had to distill them into one word, it would be time. I know that my kids, like my friend's daughter, benefitted hugely from the simple availability of time. As small children they had time to play, spending hours with blocks, with books, with paint and pencil and paper, with music, with cooking, with our ducks, with the beach and the park and the woods. Passions showed up early, some obviously, some more subtly.

By the time my son was a teenager, he loved critters and folk music. He spent time reading as much as he could about animals, especially mustelids (the weasel family) and birds. He developed relationships with adult birders in the area and went on weekend outings with them. He soaked up their knowledge, while they appreciated the sharpness of his young eyes and his enthusiasm for something they loved. He landed a job at the science museum's live animal center, doing everything from cleaning cages to feeding the snakes to holding the great horned owl for educational programs. He spent hours at the nearby folk music club, listening to music and developing relationships with the musicians and the employees before becoming a music teacher and performer there himself.

Similar stories could be told about my other children, whose time led them to pursuits including jazz, psychology, theater, and Shakespeare.

When we think about this, it makes perfect sense. Don't we all benefit from having time to do what we love? Doesn't that allow us to improve, to discover, to evolve, and to learn?

Giving kids the gift of time doesn't just fulfill their hearts and minds. Along the way, they learn valuable skills. Having available time means figuring out how to fill and manage it, so kids become self-sufficient instead of dependent on waiting for someone to tell them what to do. They learn to prioritize, to say yes to what's important or necessary, and say no to what isn't for them. Time to be alone gives kids a chance to rest, regroup, ponder, imagine, and get to know themselves.

Sometimes, the availability of time that homeschooling offers is criticized. When a homeschooler excels, people brush it off, or worse, claim unfairness, because the homeschooler had more time to devote to honing a particular skill. Yes, that's true, and what's wrong with that? Isn't time to work on things they care about something we want for all kids?

Some may fear that giving children ample time to pursue their interests could take away from their learning "the basics" and hamper their ability to get into college or get jobs. The good news is that it doesn't. The organizational, problem solving, and critical thinking skills my kids began to master through play got applied to serious studies and pursuits later on. Involvement in the community, exposure to a wide range of subjects, and observing adults in the wider world were important pieces of that process.

As I've observed my kids grow up, seeing how each of them uses their time has been fascinating, enlightening, and sometimes frustrating. One of my kids possessed a learning style that involved the obsessive embrace of one passion only to drop it for the next exciting endeavor on the horizon. Another child appeared to have a kind of tunnel vision, focusing intently on one interest to what appeared to be the exclusion of everything else. Neither of these approaches to learning match mine, which meant I had to open my mind to new possibilities, and hang tight to the belief that what my kids were doing was right for them.

It can be hard sometimes, to trust our kids' instincts, abilities, and competence. Society puts pressure on parents, and when we choose to homeschool we can feel that even more. Our own schooling experiences and social messages about how kids learn inevitably affect how we approach homeschooling, too, but when we put those things aside, the results can sometimes seem like magic. It can be hard to believe, for instance, even as it's happening right before our eyes, that kids can learn to read and multiply and write without the involvement of any teacher or boxed curriculum.

Through the challenges, I've tried my best to act as a guide and throw out ideas I think my kids might not have thought of while taking a deep breath and trusting them. I've given them the time, after all, to know themselves, and I've found that also means they know when to reach out and ask for help. They know the value of time, its gifts, its challenges, and its limitations. And that, like time itself, is precious.

Benign Neglect

I was chatting with a fellow homeschooling mom the other day, one who regularly talks to newbies looking for support. Midway into one of those conversations, she realized the suggestions she was offering might seem—well, a little neglectful.

I laughed, knowing just what she meant. I sometimes find myself casually announcing that I did zilch to teach my kids to read, and that I don't bother monitoring their writing. When I see the surprised looks, or hear the silence on the other end of the phone, I am reminded that the way I homeschool runs counter to the conventional wisdom about how to educate children.

That doesn't change the fact that letting kids freely play, explore, question, and experience life works.

However loosey goosey this may sound, it is not hands-off parenting. Just the opposite. It entails close involvement with your kids, and keen and caring observation. We watch to see what our kids care about, what they're curious about, and what they do. We help them find materials, make suggestions for activities we think would be a good fit, answer their questions, and talk to them about things we think are important.

When kids enter the teen years, the particulars may change, but the song remains the same. Kids transitioning toward adulthood still need freedom to learn and grow, and they still need our guidance.

We can give them the independence to find volunteer positions or jobs, choose community college courses (and get to them on their own), launch independent projects, attend cultural and social events, and research options for college and work. My husband and I trust our teenage daughters' innate intelligence and abilities as much as ever, but we continue to guide them by offering choices, talking, negotiating, and acting as models.

So no, I'm not being neglectful when I say I haven't seen anything my kids have written in a while, or mention that I'm not sure what they're reading right now, or remark that I have no idea what they've been quietly working on all morning.

My eyes are on the big picture, not the small potatoes. I'm aiming for intangibles like critical thinking, love of learning, and involvement in the world rather than a folder full of schoolwork. I'm watching, with awe, fascination, and love, the miraculous process of my kids growing up.

Owning It

It was tech week for *Romeo and Juliet*, and the teen that was supposed to sit at the ticket table couldn't make it.

Enter a mom to help out.

This mom, while stocking the refreshment table, overheard the following remark.

Friar Laurence to Romeo: 'We really need a kid to sell tickets.'

My gut reaction of *hey-whaddaya-mean-we-grown-ups-count-too* was as fleeting as the wink of an eye, and about as ironic. Wasn't this what all the homeschooling stuff was about, anyway? Confidence, independence, and things of that ilk?

On the website for Youthquake Theater, they claim the following: '*We are proud to say that our productions are organized, acted, and directed entirely by children and teens.*' I've been around for all of their shows, and can unreservedly say they're not exaggerating. Grown-up involvement is limited to transporting actors to rehearsals and performances, and selling tickets and refreshments.

We also get to watch, with great pleasure, the process of kids taking ownership of their work. Although I've seen it in many forms over the years, it never fails to elicit a kind of transcendent astonishment, a feeling of being surprised but not surprised, a sense of excitement as I watch what I know to *be* true—that kids are brilliant and capable —*come* true.

The ability to own their work isn't limited to kids who are homeschooled, but they're in a better position to do it than kids who spend their days being told what to do, how to do it, and whether they're good enough.

I've watched my own kids, as teens, become competent songwriters, play in professional musical ensembles, co-author psychological research, record CDs, sell art work at fairs and open studios, start a theater company specializing in the work of William Shakespeare, write and edit professionally, tutor grade school kids in math, answer phones at a suicide hotline, build websites for their various undertakings, and pursue academic subjects of their choice with zeal. I've been privileged to see other teens embrace their work with dedication and competence, too. I think what I've observed is reflective of what all teenagers, who we now know are in a period of intense, powerful brain development, can accomplish.

Lest anyone think a high-powered childhood led up to my kids' high level of productivity and drive, let me burst that bubble right now. The first decade of their lives was spent, primarily, in play. They played when they wanted to, and how they wanted to. They had ownership of their play, just as they have ownership of the work they do now.

When kids grow up with ownership of their own work (and that includes play), they are less likely to feel trapped, hopeless, isolated, and lonely. They are more likely to be able to flow with change, see challenge as opportunity, and experience satisfaction from within, rather than seeking it from without. They are more likely to be blessed with, in the words of the late, great John Holt, *'A life worth living, and work worth doing…'*[3]

[3] Instead of Education: Ways to Help People Do Things Better, John Holt

How's School?

Recently at a doctor's appointment, my daughter got the oh-so-familiar question: "How's school?"

Without skipping a beat, she replied "Great!"

The doctor asked what classes she liked. "Well," she said, "I'm enjoying history right now." The doctor said that she, not surprisingly, had really liked anatomy. The routine appointment continued, as did the pleasant conversation, which covered the delights of passionate teachers and the joys of dissecting frogs. This doctor had no idea that my daughter is homeschooled, and apparently, my daughter didn't feel the need to enlighten her.

Thinking about it later, I saw the sense in it. Most people think of school as a building one goes to every day, but with the growth of homeschooling and other forms of alternative education, that paradigm is changing. Instead of responding with an answer that negated the doctor's question, my daughter gave an answer about her current personal experience with education.

Recently, I read an article that quoted the late Paul Goodman: "Suppose you had the revolution you are talking and dreaming about. Suppose your side had won, and you had the kind of society you wanted. How would you live, you personally, in that society? Start living that way now! Whatever you would do then, do it now."

When it comes to education, the revolutionary outcome I would like to see is a world in which alternative forms of education are socially accepted. A world that recognizes the folly of one-size-fits-all education, and that supports multiple approaches. That morning, when my homeschooling daughter answered the "How's school?" question, she was living in that society. She and the doctor weren't two people on opposite sides of a fence. As each shared the common experience of a love of learning, they connected.

Such connections can only help create a world in which homeschooling and other forms of alternative education are as commonplace as a yellow school bus, no debate or discussion required, only living and learning.

The Power of Self-Identification

She wants everyone to know that she is also a farmer, mountain climber, artist, and cook.

That's the last sentence of a program biography written (well, dictated actually) many years ago by my daughter. She was four at the time, and the music director of our family's intergenerational chorus had asked her to be a page in a college production of *As You Like It*. She said yes. I was concerned that she might not fully understand the commitment, and told the music director I wouldn't force her to continue if she withdrew consent at any point. He accepted the terms, but as it turned out, my daughter felt completely at home on stage, backstage, and everywhere in between.

Now, at 18, she's turned the corner into adulthood and is a sophomore in college. The other day a visiting friend reminded me about that program bio of old and its innocent, youthful swagger. The contents made an impression on him.

What gave my daughter the confidence to self-identify in so many roles? At the time, she was my husband's right-hand helper in the garden. They were digging their green thumbs into the soil, growing tomatoes, lettuce, and other vegetables. Therefore, a farmer. We took her hiking as often as possible, and scaled plenty of large hills which she apparently interpreted as mountains. She and her siblings spent many hours using the paints, brushes, pastels, and other art supplies strewn around the house, so artist was a no brainer. When she wanted to make her own breakfast, my husband and I didn't keep her away from the stove. She'd crack the eggs, whisk them, and stand on a chair to preside over the scrambled eggs. So yeah, she was a cook, too.

Fortunately, she hasn't lost the perception of herself as a competent human being. She's always been encouraged to try things out, experiment, and explore her interests. No one told her a cook or an artist had to have credentials other than the simple act of engagement. So many of us are afraid to call ourselves what we want to be for fear that we're not adequately qualified. I wonder, sometimes, how much that holds us back.

In my role as a facilitator of creative writing groups for homeschoolers, one of my most important goals is that the kids think of themselves as writers. And why not? They come to our weekly gatherings, they participate in writing exercises, and they share their own pieces as they choose. It's not about trying to get to a point where they're good enough to have an outside authority bestow on them the title of *writer*. Their own self-identification as writers, and their investment in that self-identification, is what makes them strive to improve.

I've seen it again and again over the years. When kids have the freedom to self-identify and self-evaluate, they become confident, interested, engaged, and daring. They create, they invent, they learn. They don't have to wait until they grow up to become. They already are.

Sibling Harmony

I lead a creative writing workshop for homeschooled kids, and two of its members are sisters. It's pretty endearing to see the way they cheer each other on, support each other's work, and just generally adore each other. When one brings a story to share, her sister's eyes light up. When the story is read, there is enthusiastic applause. The love goes both ways.

In a culture where rivalry and discord are assumed inevitabilities of the sibling relationship, what I've described might seem like an anomaly. It's not an anomaly among homeschooling families. Homeschooled siblings are often close, supportive friends. Instead of spending the majority of their days apart from each other, in separate classrooms, and sometimes even separate schools, they grow up working, playing, and solving problems together. They bond.

I've seen the closeness my own kids developed as young children carry on into adolescence and adulthood. Much of this has to do with the time they're able to spend together, but there are probably other factors involved. There's no peer pressure from schoolmates telling them it's uncool to spend time with a little brother or sister. Homeschoolers are not regularly judged and evaluated by education professionals, and hence are less likely to look outside themselves for validation and compare themselves to their siblings. A homeschooling lifestyle is simply less stressful for kids, and less stress means more peace and joy in any family.

Does all this mean jealousy, bickering, and spats are nonexistent? Of course not. Homeschooling isn't perfect, but it is a lifestyle that allows siblings to really know and appreciate each other, warts and all. Disagreements are opportunities to work through issues, and doing that successfully teaches tolerance and deepens relationships.

Solitude

This is a typical day around my house: I'm working in my office, and both teenagers are in their rooms doing whatever it is they need to do. I have a vague idea of what that is — homework, writing papers and articles, preparing auditions, getting ready for upcoming performances and commitments.

Really, though, they could just as easily be reading a book that has nothing to do with work or school requirements, writing in a journal, listening to music, drawing, daydreaming, or sleeping. I don't really know, and that's the point.

Time alone is valuable, and it can be hard to come by in the frenetic pace of modern life. We are blessed to live in a bustling city with oodles of opportunities, but that doesn't negate the need for rest, renewal, and reflection. I've seen plenty of homeschooling families (including my own), miscalculate and burn out on overscheduling. One of the gifts of homeschooling is the ability to bring our schedules back into balance, and get that much needed solitude back into our lives.

I have a few extroverted children, and one introvert, and solitude has helped all of them. Self-knowledge, relaxation, idea percolation, creativity, and overall health and well-being are all fostered by solitude. Thoreau knew it, Einstein knew it, and so do you, because it's hard-wired in all of us.

Solitude for kids and teens is underrated, but their humanity cries out for private time as much as any adult. So when your kids are just hanging out, in their rooms, in the backyard, on a walk through the neighborhood, doing nothing much that you can see, just think about the importance of solitude, and the possibilities of things they're incubating: Ideas. Others. Peace. Being happy. Themselves.

Or just keep this Franz Kafka quote nearby: *You need not leave your room. Remain sitting at your table and listen. You need not even listen, simply wait, just learn to become quiet, and still, and solitary. The world will freely offer itself to you to be unmasked. It has no choice; it will roll in ecstasy at your feet.*

Give your kids have their solitude, grab some for yourself, and let the world start rolling.

What? You're a TEENAGER??

Recently my teenage daughter and I listened to someone give a dry run of a speech about education. The speaker talked about his experiences teaching at a public high school. When he finished, my daughter, as one of the teens in the audience, was asked for her feedback.

She explained that since she doesn't go to high school, she had no direct experience with the specific details in the speech. "I do take classes at community colleges, though," she continued, "They don't know how old I am, so they just treat me like the rest of the adult students, and I like that."

I wondered whether the assembled adults would absorb the profundity of that statement. Homeschooled teens have the opportunity to enroll in advanced classes, get jobs, volunteer, or otherwise function as adults out in the world. Time and again, I've seen my own kids and others rise to the challenge with flying colors.

When the kids are outed as kids, the adults are inevitably surprised and impressed. But here's the thing. In the kids' minds, they're not rising to any sort of challenge, they're just pursuing something they care about, without the impediment of any pre-conceived notions about what they're capable of because of their age.

So often when I hear people talk about education, whether it's school professionals or homeschooling parents, the emphasis is on how to make students do or learn particular things. What materials will bring out the best in them? What methods will get them to learn what we think they need to learn? What if all these methods and materials are actually obstacles in our kids' way? What if we cleared the path and let them lead? What if we believed in them enough to send them out into the world to pursue what they care about?

Believing in the competence of teens to learn, work, and make meaningful contributions can be a challenge in our culture, which tends to portray teens as lazy, immature, and sometimes even scary, but the rewards, for all of us, are immeasurable.

Where'd You Learn That?

Yesterday my daughter and I were in the car, on our way to see her sibling in a play. She's in college now, but still lives locally, so we can do things like that.

While my daughter sat beside me in the passenger seat, she worked on a paper. As she busily typed away on her laptop, I noticed something.

"Wow," I said. "You're a really fast typist." She wasn't using a two-finger method, or any other self-created style. She was typing the way I was taught to type when I was in public high school, and they offered classes for such things. Curious, I asked, "Where'd you learn that?"

"From a program I found a while ago."

"Oh," I said. "I don't remember that."

"Yeah," she said. "I wanted to learn to type so I found a typing program."

"How old were you?" I asked.

My daughter shrugged. "12 or so."

I tell this story at the risk of being accused of not paying attention, and there's some truth in that. I wasn't paying attention to how she learned to type. I did know that as a teen she was using keyboards to write papers for classes she chose to take. I didn't stand over her while she did so, and didn't concern myself with how she typed. It ain't rocket science, after all.

Although a two-finger or other makeshift method is just as useful (I have other children whose fingers move like lightning over the keyboard with their self-styled typing techniques), this kid apparently wanted something else. So she got it, on her own, and without my knowledge.

I know other homeschooling parents have experienced this. I've heard their stories, and I have others, too. For example, I have no idea how my son taught himself to make websites when he was a teenager. I have no idea how my youngest daughter learned to crochet.

Sometimes, I do know how my kids learned things, even though I had nothing to do with it. I know that my son learned about birds by going bird watching every weekend. I know that my daughter learned how to sing jazz by intensively listening to Ella Fitzgerald and other vocalists, as well as Miles Davis and other great horn players (I remember her telling me that Ella said that's what she did, listened to the horns).

One question homeschooling and unschooling parents get a lot is, "How do you know they're learning?" It's a hard question to answer. Typical attempts include pointing out children's curiosity, the human drive to learn, or trusting children.

Words inevitably fall short. When you've watched your children excitedly pursue knowledge and expertise, when you've seen them master skills on their own, when you've observed them find resources when necessary (and yes, sometimes that resource is you), the question "How do you know they're learning" becomes patently absurd. You know they're learning like you know they're breathing.

Sometimes when people ask that question, I think what they're really asking is, "How do you know *what* they're learning?" Because isn't that what school does? Tells kids what to to learn and keeps track of whether they learned it?

I plead guilty to not always keeping track of what my kids learned. I knew my kids were breathing, and I knew they were learning. Most importantly, I knew they were self-sufficient, resourceful, and empowered to learn. That's the prize I kept my eyes on.

Self-Awareness and Resiliency

Recently my daughter, who is currently studying psychology, attended an all-day seminar on resiliency in children. Afterward, she noted self-awareness as a contributing quality.

I hadn't thought much about self-awareness in the context of resiliency, but it makes sense. Being self-aware helps us understand our strengths, work on our weaknesses, and relate to others more successfully. It helps us get through rough patches, and even avoid them sometimes.

Homeschooling can contribute to the development of self-awareness in significant ways. Play, something for which homeschoolers have ample time, is a vital tool for interpreting and understanding the world and oneself. My kids and their friends set up a whole world called Little People Land, complete with a mayor and other important community members. Much happened in the seemingly endless hours they spent there. In the context of that complex social structure, they learned a great deal about themselves and others.

Real-life social interaction plays an important role in the development of self-awareness, too. By watching and relating to others, we learn that not everyone is like us, and we discover things about ourselves. Homeschooling, with its opportunities for age-mixing, finding mentors, and spending time in the community, offers kids a diverse socialization palette.

Spending time alone, to process, unwind, think, and relax, is just as necessary. Fortunately, homeschooling allows plenty of room for solitude and self-reflection.

Children who grow up deciding for themselves how to spend much of their time are more likely to know themselves. They know what they enjoy, what's not so much fun for them, what comes easy, and what doesn't. I rarely heard my kids utter that infamous refrain, *I'm bored*. Life is too full of cool things to do, and boredom, when it does occur, is just a signal to pursue a new direction.

In the absence of authorities judging and/or grading their work, homeschoolers enjoy freedom to experiment, taking risks and opening doors to experiences they might never have had the confidence or courage to try otherwise. They understand that they are in charge of their own lives, and with that privilege and responsibility, they become the foremost authorities on their own goals, conduct, and abilities.

Self-awareness also acts as a buffer to criticism, making it useful rather than discouraging. When young people are aware of their own abilities, they know when they need help, and how to seek it. They respond to criticism that contributes to positive growth, and don't take to heart negative judgments offering no path to improvement.

In Defense of Passion

Passion: a strong feeling of enthusiasm or excitement for something or about doing something—Merriam-Webster

I like passion. I mean, is that weird? Doesn't everyone like to feel enthusiastic and excited about what they do? As a parent, I like it when my kids are engaged in activities they feel passionate about. In fact, a major focus of my homeschooling style has been to help my kids find their passions, and to nurture them.

Then I read an article about how the push for passion harms kids. *Harms* kids? Have I been *harming* my kids?

Seems like passion has become a buzzword of sorts, the latest trick for getting into the college of your choice and embarking on a happily-ever-after life of achievement and success.

Maybe it's because I've been blissfully homeschooling all these years, but I missed that memo. I still think of passion as that feeling of excitement, the one that drives you to work, to experiment, to try, to learn, and as a result, to grow. I get what people say about "passion pushers," but supporting kids when they show an interest in something isn't the same as pushing. There's a fine line, you may say, and I agree. I found that when I miscalculated and crossed it, I got the *back off, Mom* message loud and clear from my kids.

Like many people, my garage and attic are full of stuff. There are the unicycles my kids used to constantly ride, the juggling clubs my son enjoyed for a couple of years, and remnants of his former obsession with birding and nature photography. The cast-off stuff isn't limited to the kids. There's also the tandem bicycle my husband bought when he used to bike our daughters around town, the Italian tapes I purchased when I decided to learn the language, and a bunch of camping gear that we don't use very much anymore. To me, these things are evidence of the rich, full lives we are fortunate enough to lead. The fact that my son no longer juggles or takes pictures of birds doesn't take anything away from the value those activities added to his life while he was doing them. The fact that the unicycles are currently collecting dust in no way diminishes the joy (not to mention exercise) they gave my daughters during the time they were riding them all over the neighborhood.

In fact, my kids have cycled through a lot of passions. Besides the aforementioned unicycling, juggling, birding, and nature photography, there were Legos, mustelids, basketball, soccer, fantasy novels, jazz, folk music, psychology, politics, neuroanatomy, Shakespeare, *Moby-Dick*, and theater.

Sometimes my kids pursue their passions like rocks along the stream of life, hopping from one to the next with glee, and sometimes they hold steady to one or two, making them roots from which to grow the rest of their lives. If pursuits are abandoned, some might say, then they're not really passions. I disagree, because here's the thing about passion. It's about the present, not the future. It's about learning and embracing in the moment. Sometimes that leads to the formation of long-term goals, and sometimes it doesn't. In order to avoid pushing our kids, that's something we have to accept. Quitting happens, and it doesn't necessarily signal wasted time or effort.

How else to avoid pushing? Value the process, not the product. Expose your kids to lots of subjects and activities, but don't jump every time you perceive an interest—if they want to pursue something, they'll let you know. Perhaps most important of all, be a model, and live your own life with passion.

Peace + Park Day

What is it about park day?

The other night a homeschooling mom was telling me about her first time attending a local park day for young children. Several older kids came, and the play turned rough.

As the new kid on the block, she thought staying quiet was best. But as a mom, she decided to broach the subject. She told me that her questions were met with lectures and dismissal. She left feeling judged, and she hasn't gone back.

As she related her experience, I nodded my head in recognition. Over more than two decades of homeschooling, I've seen way too many rifts over park days.

Seriously? Fights over going to the playground?

It may sound ridiculous, but park day can be sacred. For many support groups, it serves as the glue that holds the community together. It's the place where families go regularly to gather, play, socialize, and forge connections. It's also where new homeschoolers go, often enthusiastically, but sometimes tentatively, as an entry point to the brave new world they've decided to inhabit.

I don't mean to imply that park days create more problems than they're worth. They don't. Park days are a beautiful thing, and many of my fondest memories involve sunny days laughing around picnic tables, dipping toes in the brook, watching games of ultimate frisbee and kickball, and engaging in spirited discussion with other adults.

But like every situation where people gather in groups, agreement is not always a given. I wasn't present at the above scenario, but maybe the parents whose kids were playing so rambunctiously felt they had to defend their choices, or their certainty about the value of their children's play obscured their ability to hear another's concerns. One thing I'm pretty sure of is that they didn't intend to make anyone feel unheard or unsafe, but unfortunately, that is what happened. "All I wanted was to talk about it," the mom who shared her story said.

Simple, and yet so, so difficult.

The story put me in mind of something I heard at a neighborhood event I recently attended. "Community," someone said, "is where the person you least want to be there, is."

We like to think about community through rose-colored glasses, as some idyllic, utopian existence where everyone gets along every minute of every day. The truth is, being in relationship with others is messy. When we venture into groups, it's inevitable that we'll encounter people we don't agree with. Maybe we don't like their views, or their parenting styles, or the clothes they wear, or the way they talk. When this happens, learning to peacefully coexist can be a challenge, especially in homeschooling support groups where there's often no clear leader or defined decision-making process. Throw in the fact that homeschoolers, by nature, tend to be strong-willed folk with strong opinions, and it can make navigating a support group feel a bit like stepping into the wild west.

This makes it even more important to listen to each other as best we can, and be open to compromise and change. Sometimes, we'll reach agreement. Other times, we'll agree to disagree. Still other times, we'll part ways. If we're really lucky, we may see each other clearly, and the person that was the one we least wanted to be there, becomes one we couldn't imagine living without.

On Not Teaching Kids to Read

I was very glad the other day to discover an excellent essay by Carol Black[4]. Black is a visionary writer on education and learning, and deserves a large readership.

Black says, "...people today do not even know what children are actually ***like.*** They only know what children are like ***in schools."***

I remember having a similar revelation when my eldest daughter was about twelve. In response to a discussion on developmental issues, her pediatrician xeroxed a section of a book on child psychology for me to study. That night as I flipped through the pages and read all about what was "normal," it couldn't have been more clear to me that the "normal" that was being presented was based almost entirely on children who live the majority of their days inside a school building. Hence, it wasn't particularly relevant for me or my children.

---

[4] A Thousand Rivers: What the Modern World Has Forgotten About Children and Learning, Carol Black, http://carolblack.org/a-thousand-rivers

Black's piece also got me thinking about my children's experiences learning to read. My eldest spent a year in kindergarten before I decided to homeschool. As a socially oriented child, she wanted to please and impress the teacher, and was keenly aware of what would be necessary to reach a high status in the classroom (one of the many reasons, actually, I turned to homeschooling, but that's another story).

Only one child in her class was reading, and this made him special. My daughter came home, sat herself down on the couch, and told me she wanted to read. "Okay," I said, and proceeded to do my best to help her sound out words. She was pretty good at phonics at that point, and could sound out individual phonemes, but putting them together was another matter. We spent many painful hours in which she would try her hardest, reciting "c-uh," "a," "tuh," but lacking whatever cognitive mechanism was required to merge those sounds into the word "cat."

Eventually, of course, she learned to read. Did all the phonics hullabaloo facilitate it? I doubt it.

Not long after, my kids' father and I got divorced, and off they went to school for a couple of years. My son entered a one/two classroom (first and second grade) in an alternative school full of earthy crunchy, liberal families. He hadn't gone to kindergarten, and his reading ability was nonexistent.

Even in this progressive environment, the pressure the children felt to read in first grade was enormous. My son felt none of this. His teacher, who lamented the worries these six and seven year-olds already had about their abilities, would tell me what a wonderful example my son was for the rest of the class. "I can't read, can somebody help me?" he would ask. His openness made him a target for ridicule, and his reading level, or lack thereof, made him a candidate for special time with the resource teacher.

During the summer between first and second grade, he forgot about school and played. One day in July, I walked into his room and he was reading Roald Dahl's "Fantastic Mr. Fox."

He went back to second grade, and in October his classroom teacher called to tell me he no longer needed time with the resource teacher. He had been tested, she told me, and was reading at a third grade level, with a fourth grade level of vocabulary. "What did you do?" she asked me.

What I did, of course, was nothing. The teacher didn't believe me. It was inconceivable to her that my son could go from being so "behind" to being so "ahead" with no intervention.

But wait, some might argue, it was the hours he spent in school, and the time he had with the resource teacher, finally kicking in. Without that, maybe he wouldn't have learned to read. Again, I doubt it (so did the teachers; the giant leap he took over the summer wasn't something they typically saw in a child already identified as a late reader).

Later, I remarried and had two more daughters, neither of whom ever attended school. We visited the library regularly and read books to them often. They also spent many hours looking at books. Formal reading instruction? There was none. If you ask me how they learned to read, I would have to tell you honestly, I don't know. They just did.

I know my kids are not special. I've observed many kids learn to read completely by themselves. As someone who's been around children who were not subjected to forced reading instruction in school, the typical curve for reading that Black describes sounds exactly right to me. Some kids might read at age three or four, others might wait until they're ten or eleven. When left alone to develop their reading skills naturally, the age is immaterial. In the long term, they will read equally well, and, as with walking and talking, no one will know or care how old they were when they started.

The repercussions that Black describes so eloquently of forcing children to learn to read before they're ready, willing, and able are real. "This is a choice," she says. "In making it, we may be creating disabilities in kids who would have been fine if allowed to learn to read on their own developmental schedule."

Fortunately, as homeschoolers, we have the option of choosing not to force, reward, or interfere with our children's developmental schedule for reading.

Do Kids Have to Go to College?

College has been on my mind lately. We're knee-deep in the application process for my third child, who hopes to attend a school of her choice in the fall. Of my four children, she's the only one who unequivocally wanted or wants to attend college. My oldest didn't go, my second quit after two years, and number four is on the fence. Does that make you pause? In a world where the conventional wisdom seems to be that college is a necessity, I wouldn't be surprised. Just last week, the New York Times published a piece called "Is Your First Grader College Ready?" It was meant to be provocative, but only fuels the entrenched notion that eschewing college means no chance for a successful life.

Neither of my parents had much formal education. My mother, who came to the United States in the 1950's at the age of 27, left school when she was 11 because she was needed at home. There were zero books in her house, and precious few in her tiny village in the mountains of Italy. Like most people of her generation and her background, she sees education as the ticket to opportunity, economic success, and ultimately, happiness. Statistics about the earning power of those with and without college degrees seem to prove her right. And yet, the promise of college has turned into a broken dream for so many young people shouldering massive debt from student loans, and seeking difficult-to-land jobs in our rapidly-changing economy.

Despite this, most teenagers assume college is a requirement. "Where are you applying?" is a standard question for young people, most of whom are given the message by their families, schools, and the larger culture that college is expected. Somehow, I didn't get that memo. Although I loved school, including college, in raising my own kids I chose to embrace a completely different educational paradigm.

***

What about college? When it comes to the most common questions directed at homeschoolers, it's second only to *What about socialization?*

Last year when I was conducting a workshop for new homeschoolers, someone in the audience asked whether my kids got into college. Not whether my kids chose college, not what my kids were doing with their lives, but whether they were able to *get in.* I replied that my eldest didn't go to college and my second quit after two years, but my third was about to apply. Maybe I imagined the deflated look on the woman's face, but I don't think so. Homeschooling parents and others can take admission to college as evidence of success, and a job well done. A child who doesn't get into the college of their choice, or who doesn't choose college at all, can hit current or prospective homeschooling parents in an emotional weak spot. I get that. I found myself pulling my hair out when my son decided to quit college to pursue a career as a full-time folk musician. But what did I expect? He was raised unconventionally, to see possibilities beyond the beaten path.

***

Years ago, Peter Kowalke made a movie called *Grown Without Schooling*. It profiled several young adults who'd been homeschooled in the 1970s and 80s. You'd be hard pressed to find commonalities among them. The one I noticed was that they were all open, self-aware, and thoughtful about their lives and choices. For some, that didn't include college, or entrepreneurship, or traditional employment.

I attended a showing of the movie for homeschooling parents. At the post-screening discussion, it was fascinating to see how unsettled many of them were. They found it difficult to accept that each and every one of the grown homeschoolers couldn't be held up as "successes" in the eyes of society. I understand the reaction. We all want what's best for our kids. Our culture puts so much responsibility on parents for how kids "turn out," and homeschooling only magnifies that burden. But our kids are individuals, like us. There's a certain amount of irony in play when homeschooling parents expect their kids to take a traditional path. Our homeschooled children know better than we that learning doesn't have to happen in a school. They've lived it. Ultimately, they'll take the paths they choose, and if we can take a deep breath and relax, watching those paths unfold can be a learning opportunity for us.

***

Almost daily, my daughter receives glossy flyers from universities all over the country, decorated with color photos of satisfied students engaged in studious conversation, working in state-of-the-art labs, using impressive facilities. These schools are trying to sell their product, and they want to make it look as attractive as possible. The value of knowledge for its own sake, and the profound effect that deep learning experiences have in making us who we are, don't appear to be paramount. Mark Edmundson talks about this in his book *Why Teach: In Defense of a Real Education*. He says about formal schooling, "We are educated to fill roles, not to expand our minds and deepen our hearts. We are tooled to slide into a social machine and function smoothly with a little application from time to time of the right pleasing grease. Education now prepares us for a life of conformity and and workplace tedium, in exchange for which we can have our iPhones, our flat screens, our favorite tunes, Facebook and Twitter." One of the reasons I chose homeschooling was to keep my kids from sliding into the emptiness of the social machine. As a result of homeschooling, our adult children often have a broader sense of options and possibilities. They aren't machines that need to be well-oiled by social constructs. They can create, and nurture, themselves.

***

There's much to be gained from the resources available at a university (and Edmundson has much to say about this in his book), especially when the student enters with an intact love of learning. But is attendance necessary for "success" or even to become educated? I think not, and the sooner we parents get that, the better. Of course college degrees can open doors for their recipients, but it's possible to get jobs, start businesses, learn trades, and live fulfilling lives without a college degree. What's more important than any piece of paper is the process of becoming an educated person. As homeschooling parents, this is what we've offered our children. We plant the seeds and guide them when they're young, but by the time they reach college age, however they extend the process is up to them. Whether they choose college or not is immaterial to whether their education will continue. As Edmundson puts it, "...what we want is real learning—learning that will help us see the world anew and show us that there could be more to our lives than we had thought." That kind of priceless education can happen anywhere.

ACKNOWLEDGEMENTS

Eternal gratitude to my husband Glenn Dickson, and my kids. Justine McDonald, Eric McDonald, Claire Dickson, and Abby Dickson, you inspire me every day. Thanks to Sophia Sayigh for years of friendship and working together on too many projects to count. To Stephanie Griego, Morgan Kennedy Henderson, Amy Faeskorn, and Tracy Ventola, my colleagues at Advocates for Home Education in Massachusetts, I love working with you. To Pat Farenga for friendship and support over the years. To John Holt and John Taylor Gatto for life-changing inspiration. To all my homeschooling friends, it was a great ride!

ABOUT THE AUTHOR

Milva McDonald is the mother of four adult children, all of whom homeschooled for all or most of their child and teenage years. As one might expect, they are each on unique paths. Justine is a behavior specialist, a singer-songwriter, and a music teacher. Eric is a coffee connoisseur and folk musician; check him out at ericmcdonaldmusic.com. Claire is a rising junior at Harvard College majoring in psychology, and a jazz singer; check her out at www.clairedicksonmusic.com. Abby is attending University of Massachusetts Boston Honors College in the fall and loves theater and Shakespeare; check out her youth company at youthquaketheater.com.

Milva started homeschooling in 1991, after reading an essay by John Taylor Gatto and realizing school and the PTA weren't for her. For three decades she worked for *The Boston Globe* and boston.com writing and reporting about arts and cultural events in Boston. Other pursuits over the years included running a folk music coffeehouse, organizing countless field trips, facilitating creative writing groups for kids, passing hors d'oeuvres at fancy parties, and performing in several editions of *The Christmas Revels.* She sings in *The Halalisa Singers* and blogs at apotlucklife.com. She is the recipient of a 1997 Massachusetts Cultural Council Artist Grant. She and Sophia Sayigh are co-authors of the fictional book *Unschoolers*. Learn about it at unschoolersbook.com.

Printed in Great Britain
by Amazon

67881027R00056